WORDS WILL

DENNIS EDWARD HOPPER

To Mamie:

Dennis Edward Hopper

Outskirts Press, Inc.
http://www.outskirtspress.com

ISBN: 978-1-4787-5938-6

Outskirts Press and the "OP" logo are trademarks belonging to Outskirts Press, Inc.

PRINTED IN THE UNITED STATES OF AMERICA

This book is dedicated to
my wife and sons.
They make my world complete.

TABLE OF CONTENTS

A BOY'S FOREST

There was an old forest on the hill
behind the house where I lived
when I was an Addison boy.
Alone, I trod these quiet woods
imagining not another foot
had ever walked my secret paths.
Moments of fear from noise and sign
      might liven the stalk,
yet nothing, maybe just rattlers,
or maybe bears at night,
lived among my trees
(they were my trees)
      which would harm me.

My trees were lucky things
to be happy where they were.
Water at the bottom and air at the top.
Feet in the earth and head in the sun.
Ash and maple, elm and hickory,
pine and oak, apple, and even plum -
making a pungent deep shade
where a lonely boy could
roam his own giant leaf-strewn room
and drink wild spring water
and dream of leaving them.

THE SWIMSUIT AT FREEMAN BRIDGE

By taking my wrinkled credentials to the
Freeman bridge I can still slip into the mind of the
boy in the baggy black swimsuit with its old white cotton

belt which used to be his
father's alone on a large sun-warmed
rock surrounded by clear waters of a country

creek beneath. Splayed with feet and hands and
head dangling off the sides as if
fallen face down from the rusted iron span

where traffic clanked above and landed sprawled across this
pediment but doing nothing more than watching baby fish and
tadpoles hurry about in the clear

cold mountain water twitching water-bent
white fingers just to watch them investigate,
flick away and then, no wiser, hurry

back in an instant to be frightened
again. His mind floats in the enormity of its unshaped future with the
specter of time itself still beyond the

horizon not yet looming which lets young
eyes watch a fish, a bird, a tree, or
pebble completely and ask nothing of their

existence but the right to imagine in boy
words what they must think; if they think,
being what they are.

That rounded yellow stone in the water he thought
was rubbed smooth by millions of years of
service shoulder to shoulder with brother

stones doing what this stone army did, going where it went rolling,
clicking and sliding with the happy current warmly polished by friendly
contact with neighbor

stones marching proudly in an eternal downstream
parade toward some noble end; building, stacking, creating,
and together, always together, in close harmonious brotherhood.

Having crept back in to feel that sweetness, it is too soon under siege
by the consequences of too many years
passing. Now, chin resting on arthritic and aching hands on the

railing above looking back through myopic and spectacled
eyes, I know the yellow marching stone was just being abraded
to a shadow of a once larger more imposing self

and trapped in a ceaseless overpowering maelstrom of helpless rocks
(of mostly granite origin) worn by eons of chipping and grinding to
become so fragmented and

eventually disintegrated into the dull conformity of sand
and then dust, then lifeless clay, in one of the most
boring immutable processes of our physical world.

A CRY TO SUMMON THE MUSE

The true menace of this beast,
lies in the slowness with which it stalks its prey.
    No insight, sense,
or primal instinct, can prepare for a pounce
which has been decades in the making.
    There is no rumbling growl
or slap of feet or meaty breath of the hunter,
jaws agape, turned to clasp the neck
in dripping fangs.
    The prey is neither savaged nor slain
yet is still consumed, with so much essence
stolen away, by this beast called . . .
                    time.
    Is it now too late to create
by digging through the detritus
of this disintegrating core looking for usable gems?
    Can loose and flaking particles
rattling down from ancient fissured walls
metamorphose through pure desperation
into words which glide and flow?
    How do I moisten, infuse and bring
light to this aged and dessicated gourd,
to make it instead
a garden or font pouring forth
perfect expressions of treasured images
now snarled too deeply in a dense ropy tangle
of heaped cerebral trash?
    I ache to speak of golden things
with new and vivid words

and feel again cool fresh winds bursting
through long-closed creaking old gates -
blasting down dark and dusty corridors!
       God, yes. Happily spew bright new thoughts
like jets of fireworks thumping toward the sky
to flicker, flash, and bang so
wildly that minds reel and bodies flinch
in excitement and laughter!
       To feel and sense as youths again;
awash in the newness of
anger, joy, outrage, and indignation
over delicious, stunning,
revelation upon revelation!
       Please.
       Now I'm begging.
Not to remain mute still with timorous aching
and fear of revealing
a passionless heart and hiding again
in life's limitless mundanity.

(Or afraid to let strangers wander
through these cluttered caverns
ogling with incredulity through foetid air
the sickly lumps and masses
projecting from this inner fundament
like jellied purple parasitic fungi
bulging through old bark on rotting stumps.
       Who could look at such things
and abide the host?
       Who would allow such things to be seen?)

and not saying too late,
       too late;
bidding weakly with hope and resignation

for the magic which now can be seen
only through a strong lens.

     Be nice and quit complaining, I'm told.
     Time is here for dinner.

(Ah, yes, I know.
The old guy stumbles
among these little heaps
of mangled adjectives.

     But . . . to hell with it.
It's got to be better than silence.
     Go ahead and look.)

BEACH VACATION

      I do not trust the damned
ocean. I resent the laughing
waves poofing and haw-
hawing like sopping bullies faking
punches just to see me flinch.
      Too aggressive they charge
my feet, just to empty in front of me
wet hands full of dead things
and shattered and worn fragments
left over from her cruel adventures
untold years and miles away in times
so long before me even
      in other lands I'll never see.
So pretty
      yet a conniving bitch with a million-mile-long
grin showing foaming pale teeth
in often shitbrown water chomp chomping at
my dry, solid, reliable earth.

It smells like death, the sea
does, where dumb water creatures
die floating 'til their flesh is flayed
      and beaten white by sand
and salt becoming morsels for a scavenged sea
repast or flung onto the beach
      with a plop
for reptilian birds with cruel
      beaks and monotonous screeches
to peck and pull apart

while leaving white fecal smears on my sand.
That is the smell of this fungal sea
and the things it kills.
      I know.
      Oh, I know.
She will float a man high in her
sparkling arms and hold him
      up to the sun
like the triumphant midwife
      proud of the babe she pulled into life.
She will let him ride on her back
      like a youth at a gallop astride
green, white-maned prancing
water ponies joyously dragging salty
      air into defenseless
lungs while marveling at the power and
speed of this wondrous friend.
      But, I tell you.
                I tell you.
She rages beneath you.
She is always hungry.
She will eat your world.
She won't hear your prayers,
and she wants your bones to keep
deep, deep, deep
in her cold dark airless belly forever.

NOT JUST LOVE

It was not a heart, not a mind, but a cynical soul
     adrift in modern seas with no map or guide,
         rescued.
It was finding truth in a small tangle of new cells with
     needs of staggering simplicity.
Who knew that a child, a baby, would be salvation;
the savior of that soul - teaching him elemental
love while causing a wrenching rearrangement
of priorities into something totally human?
     How do I understand a feral need to touch and
smell and taste, to practically chew on arms and legs
as if only by swallowing their flesh could you
explore the depth of this feeling – this sense
that they are you and you are they – to complete
     this creation of self, a new me?
It was watching the opening of their eyes
     so wide, so empty,
so ready to be filled with the world I hand them.
It was opening my eyes wide enough finally so that this
new person could see the bald clarity of my feelings.
     I could stare and stare and stare
into this breathtaking abyss and weep at the purity
of this new universe, this pool of potential,
     this most elemental humanity,
     thrown open in defenseless adoration
whose new mind knows only hunger,
and shudder at the vastness of the
need to assure that it is safe from my ignorance.

MY SNOW MY YOUTH

New definitions of white fallen,
changing the texture of our world.
Recklessly flopping on our backs
on the ground trusting this
miracle of nature to cushion us
then make snow angels
      when we were angels
yelping with glee at moments
stolen from chores and

school racing down once
ordinary slopes bravely
grinning, red-faced, runny-nosed,
and wet with ice-hardened
clothes and cold-stiffened
fingers in worn out mittens
but unwilling to give up

the magic of rolling and falling
with fellow heroes daring brave tumbles
in forgiving frozen softness
      of the new snowfall
and even eating with feral hunger
the cushions on which we played.
Nothing else in life will ever be
as pure as this snow, this thirst.

Then, in the dark early winter morning
it is air freezing itself again. Up from
the warm cocoon of the old quilted bed,
cold on your face, back to school,
kicking your way through glittering crystals
on a pale white morning world lit
by the frosty blue silver of
the hard winter moon
healing yesterday's slashes
overnight, piling flake upon
flake with a miniature rattle of ice on ice
reduced to a serene hiss
            if you listen carefully
        leaving only the gentlest hollows over
proof of yesterday's joy.

WAR BRAINS

You say this
I say that
Therefore you must die.

   You believe this
   I believe that
   Therefore I must kill you.

     You did this
     I did that
     Therefore we are dead.

DEBT

I stumble along this rutted road; deep
lines cut in sticky mud by
heavy loads borne by tired souls
on a thousand aching feet
who could not lay down their burden,
who could not stop . . .
        who could not rest
in the eternal cruel mist from
leaden skies
yet in their endless plodding
        made a path for me.

Raising my strained and self-absorbed brow;
finally lifting my eyes from clotted shoes;
pointing my face instead toward the
distant point where all
their muddy tracks converge . . .
I see blue.

HOW?

I knew a man who put tags on toes
of the bodies of friends
      now just dead in war.
I knew a man who stalked among
the enemy who had fallen to make sure
      that none would rise again.
I knew a man who killed a man
because his arms were too low
      in surrender.
I knew a man who helped build a bomb
which left mere shadows on stone
      from humans vaporized.
And I knew a man who ran into a
storm of hissing bullets and felt guilty
      that none had killed him.
What I did not know was that
brave men would weep from a pain
      so old, so buried,
        borne silently and so unfairly
        as penance for the act of living.
I did not know that such sorrow
could dwell so deep . . so sore
      still.

POLITICAL POLLSTER ON THE PHONE

Thoughts?
He wants my thoughts?
Sure he can have them . . .
        all of them.

I'm tired of my thoughts.
I don't want most of them any more.
I've got too many and
I can't use them all.
I had some real good ones,
        once;
Like the difference between a
John Deere and a Farmall.
Or a Ford versus a Chevy.
But, now they just take up room.
        I need to downsize.
Oh, I'll keep the ones on love.
I'll keep friendship and family.
        On this you can rely.
(An old song. You wouldn't know it.)
        The fundamental things apply.
Sorry, I'm flashing back.

Your man? The one who's running?
        He's a nitwit -
but, sure, he can have my thoughts.
        Send him by the house.
I'll give him ten right off,
maybe twenty, if he's got the time.
He just has to promise to
        take all of them.
I don't even want those big ones;
the ones which stirred my passions when
        I was young;
like the ones on politics,
        war, or religion.   .
I tried to put one on the other day.
I think it was the one on unions.
It just don't fit any more.
It was a little tight in the seat.
        Sure, tell him to come on by.

OLD FACTORY

At just the right time,
when blue smoke seemed thickest
white sunlight would burst through
small holes in the black dirt on old ceiling glass

panes slashing a long way down through the
darkness of the giant room
making brilliant widening shafts
in the oily haze of the brightest blue

light moving sideways
starring spindle, table, shaft, gear,
perhaps a face, for a few minutes a day
then up a wall and away.

Dirty men at oil wet machines did not look up.
Piece rate pay. Paid by how many they finished.
Pushing hard in small pools of yellow

light with just enough bulb for their
work, men set the piece, popped
in the tool, pushed "on" and
watched as rough metal in puddles of

lustrous green oil was turned or
ground or drilled or milled or
cut smooth and polished ready to
fit in its place while around them the room is

screaming with the brain-piercing screech
of a too-fast cut in iron gone dry
and a dull tool's angry chatter along with the
church bell clang of a heavy steel

hammer on huge iron casting and
endless smoky roar of
tow motors bringing new pallets of work
to be done. Men spoke in

shouts, sucking misted oil, iron dust,
and smoke into lungs which wouldn't feel the
lethality of these deadly inhalations until too

late. It never yields. Twenty-four hours,
three shifts, it roars and consumes metal and men.
Moments of laughter and yelping of grown men

goosing, playing grab-ass, as they obey the whistle and
dented tin pails rattle open for a drink and
quick sandwich dashed to the mouth with black-nailed fingers
while machines whine and demand their return.

Days and weeks go on and on
as years pass by the time clock door
and the factory gives them money and poisoned blue air
in exchange for their youth.

DEVICES PLOT

Piz awoke and rolled out of the stack of mole furs and dropped twenty feet to the floor, careful to avoid the dripping pointed spikes above. He strode carefully across the steeply slanted stone platform the edge of which dropped off hundreds of feet to the molten lava below. He was hobbled by the still raw bullet wound to the peritoneum which bled as he moved. It was in Sardinia during the Hotel caper when he had been shot by his lover from the OSS. In the middle bath room, he luckily chose the one bottle without the rat poison and stole a sip before he took the steam trolley into the street. Spotted, he ran the length of the mirrored causeway which had been designed by his children's father. He saw Eelf pull up in a variegated six-wheel Plymouth and motion with her leg for him to quickly get on top. They managed to elude the gray bucks and make it to the Samoan bakery where the buns with the messages awaited. The counterman who was Eelf's brother flicked his eye toward a clown-costumed elderly prostitute sitting on the floor holding a clutch of green beets. Piz quickly assimilated – green and beets – realizing that beets aren't green. At the moment this realization exploded in his sternum, the disguised man dropped the beets into the blue Russian ammo can which exploded with lethal forcibility. Instantly, the Slavs leaped to their bare feet and began firing Stens. Piz thought back to that time when his aunt felt his. The counterman dropped into a lidless pit in the garages concrete floor and slithered through the pipe to the station. Piz barely squeezed through a foot-wide door at the edge of the pastry case leaving a gouge in the solid gold frame from the buckle of his invisible thread trousers. Meeting in the icy alley they ran once again to the waiting Harley marveling that a woman with no legs could have moved so quickly. They raced through the castle courtyard while Piz lay atop the orange platform firing his laser pistol at the buzzing drones. He knew they wouldn't make it because the Rail hadn't told them where

Sebum buried the bonger tape and the helium was getting low. When they arrived, Piz stumbled in the darkness across the second body while carrying Eelf and would have kept crawling but Eelf quietly screamed "look!" When they had finished and Eelf had re-clothed from the passion of the moment, Piz saw the blue sign and thought for a heartbeat that they were safe. It showed the smoking word "tide." Maybe they had at last reached the fabled shore! But the word had a backward "e" and "d. " Upon further study with the calibrated scope, it looked almost as if it had somehow burned through the metal. With fear clawing at his now exposed guts like icy talons, he knew. After screaming poop, he dropped Eelf and crawled quickly to the other side of the neon sign and realized the worst had happened. Eelf stared knives with her red eye as Piz sunk to the cold deck in despair. They knew it was over. They were goners. They must die in the scorn of rewrite. Tears runneled. Still glowing on the other side of his brother's sign was lasered the ultimate horror; the last thing they were prepared for: "edit."

LAST IN CAMP

Last to leave,
I stood alone where we had lived
　　　　(It was six days fishing.)
chasing elusive memories still sparking
in a mind getting ready to
get back to the business
of life but not ready for a final farewell
　　　　before driving away
myself after my pals had left . . .
　　　　trying to preserve a complete
picture of golden moments just past,
　　　　hoping to pull something more solid
from the air I could stuff in my heart's
pockets like a favorite knife
always there.

We fished and talked, ate and argued,
slept and woke, in the easy camaraderie of
old friends for days - then left in strange
haste for homes - most far away -
recognizing one of life's most painful rules:
　　　　when it's over, it's over.

Good campers, we left nothing behind but
　　　　ashes in the fire rings
to show we had used this place
in the woods
on the lake shore so totally.

We did so much on
this dusty ground - making the emptiness
now only more bleak.
     A pennant should be flying
     at half mast
     or signatures left in a book
     on a stand outside this now
     somber green room
     where the remains
     of brotherhood lay.

     But, it's time to go.
I see the sun glows just as brightly even
     though we quit laughing
and the water in the lake
     has already forgotten us.
Only the smell of dust and a growing
vacuum surround me
     as the trees, leaves, and
winking shade casually sweep
our boisterous adventure
from the air to take back their
selfish dominion.

BAR MUSICIAN

You see them like this:
        shoulders forward,
slumped, chin down,
eyes closed tight as if in pain,
        lost in their own world,
elbows in close, hands pulled in to the body,
        almost fetal, except for fingers alive on keys
and toes on peddles, together asking this piano
to speak aloud in their language.
        It looks like they are cringing,
        as if the air might resent these sounds –
        as if the air is an enemy.
        They stroke the keys
to create a noise resonating   just so
        around them . . .
        each note an echo of another first played
in their minds and shaped by a desire
for one perfect tonal birth after another.
        Music is forged in this
        lonely human crucible
amid often comic contortions.
        How do you watch a
man twisted in this awkward passion?
        This hope is too intense,
too obvious - somehow desperate -
that the creation is first perfect here
before it is borne from this
chord shaped womb
by the anxious parent and

set with tremulous
hands like a bloody damned sacrifice
of flesh placed so outrageously
among beer and pretzels
gobbled by louts with cash who,
indifferent, continue to
munch, talk, and laugh
about truly ordinary things
not looking, not hearing
at all, this creation raining
melodic pearls and rubies
from the air around them.

Again and again he will
suffer this intensely
personal, laborious,
uniquely public birth,
with the almost pitiful
wish that this unworthy audience
finds his children beautiful.

WHISKEY HAMMER

hey there whiskey hammer
no matter malt or rye
keep raining those soft sweet blows
on strength
will
duty
watch me dance a jig
forget promises
lost in the little amber mirror
where I always
find myself handsome

TODAY'S ENEMIES

The new battlefield
finds no way to
counter the poisonous pellet
lodged in the brain of the
enemy when he was a child and
      still today leaking venom.

Or remove the rusted nails of hatred
fallen on as youths and
lodged near those hearts
creating necrotic masses
infecting souls of whole generations
who would die
for the chance to kill you.

WILLIE'S LAMENT

I had to laugh at this sorrowful feeling
I ran so fast while all the time kneeling
I've slowly climbed to the bottom of the rope
I've found the beginning of the loss of hope
Even the blind can plainly see
I can't breathe
I can't see
I ain't here
This ain't me
This ain't me
I ain't here
I can't see
I can't breathe
Even the blind can plainly see
I've found the beginning of the loss of hope
I've slowly climbed to the bottom of the rope
I ran so fast while all the time kneeling
I had to laugh at this sorrowful feeling

BOOM TOWN ROAD

Once a proud, dark slash on the land,
flat, smooth and black, crushed stone immersed and
glued in viscid remnants of dinosaurs and ferns, pressed
and painted by dirty men in yellow machines.

Along its middle and flanks, glowing white streaks and yellow
dashes demand in stark contrast
to a softer countryside declaring its
lawful authority guiding the eye and wheel of the
wayfarer across long miles of the best countryside taken by
edict from crops and pasture
to cut shallow trenches in native soil
for pavement, shoulders and ditches.

Once, with great confidence,
it insisted that travelers go this way, or just the opposite,
that way, obeying the bossy
lines carefully drawn exactly down the
middle to keep the speeding hulks from touching one
another or from wandering off the permitted path.

The storied mine died long before the road
leaving the once busy path unrenewed, then abandoned,
to fade to paler and paler gray with volatile tars and reasons to
persist burnt away by years in the open oven of the sun;

no lines, directing nothing, going nowhere, just drying and shrinking.
Cracks spreading like lightening strokes
open the road to patient seeds and little weeds
which, in all the world
know best how to survive our mistakes.

IDA MUSTON'S PRIZE

The work of Ida's hands hangs still
in the gloom of the old Muston
house under rough shake roof,
listing badly in the sea of years - sagging
hopelessly under the weight of
time and bricks from the collapsed
          chimney strewn heavily across
steadily weakening timbers.

The seasons sneak in through jagged
holes to weaker woods planned
just for indoor
climes. Sills and joists beneath the
floor have aged past
          rotten, now soft and
          brown just like the
earth they rest on . . . soon to be earth.

          A May breeze puffs
through crooked windows with broken
panes where, in a small upstairs
room, a lone tattered curtain still
hangs by a few stubborn threads on rusted
          rod softening the
light with the yellowness of its
age, sweeping its frail speckled shadow
lightly across the slanted
floor which once boldly sported
large purple and black flowers on linoleum
          vivid even in gaslight.

So fragile, so old; the lace of the curtains,
which took First at the county fair,
was the issue of Ida's hands;
the young ones which made
them and old ones which patched
them, never suspecting
a thing made with such love -
which had seen so much love -
could be this alone.

The ragged knots and linen whisper
quietly in concert with a faintly huffing breeze
        and Ida's prize weaves and bends,
gently flicking frayed
        ends in a tired shuffle . . .
an endless last dance
to the music of time and the wind.

THE HIGH COST OF LIVING

Too long I careened through life,
dancing atop a runaway train
drinking the wind in my face
like another fine wine
on exciting night rides
on a long smooth road with no exits,
excited at flashing lights whipping by
yet blinded to the steady welcoming glow
of lamps where friends dwelled
beckoning me to quit
this pointless journey.

How many times I should have quit the ride
and embraced the love they offered
yet eagerly crawled back aboard
again and again and rode on -
still the eternal fool anxious to arrive
at a place called nowhere . . .
then ride still strutting and yipping
the other way until, finally,
too late wiser. . .
getting there.

Too late I learned the price I paid -
how deep the pain of people hurt
and how high the cost
of friendships lost.

FIRST DEATH

Yes, there was light, not white
but bright.
And the fall was a fall, not down
but up.
There was a sound, not loud
but strong
and the blackness was black, not black
but starlit.
The trip was quick, not short
but fast
and the memory is deep, not bad
but real.
The time wasn't right, not wrong
but early.

BRACKEY'S PLACE

He lived the life of brick and stone
Where buildings loomed and streets were home
      Rock as a pillow, concrete as bed
      He slept in dirt, left spots where he bled.
He said the pears were the fruit of the day
Because that's what he stole from a stand on the way.
      He hated his hands for the look of his skin
      Always so rough with the dirt rubbed in.
He cried when a friend took a knife in the gut
And laughed when the cops locked the wrong guy up.
      Said the city was like a big, gray hearse
      He was stuck inside for better or worse.
He'd pay, he said, to ride a horse instead
In a place wide open with the sun on his head.
      He prays, he said, to feel a woman's touch
      And someone to care just a little, not much.
Brackey thought he was maybe born wrong
That where he was wasn't where he belonged.
      He sometimes felt like there was more to say
      But the words he used didn't go the right way
He thought his thoughts were often so clear
And he was going to know and the time was near
      What a man was and what it was all about
      And what he should do and how to get out.
But, it wasn't really clear and he didn't really know
He was stuck in this place with nowhere to go.
      Brackey always said it was stupid to die
      When you ain't ever lived and you don't know why.

But that's what happened as he sat on the roof
Blood pouring out and facing the truth
       He had time to yell at the world out there
       They could all go to hell and they could have his share.

PERVERSE JOY

It is there – below.
I look down in desperation.
Miles of quiet deep valleys and black
dirt bottom-lands taken by rivers, roads
and farms through verdant rolling
hills lying rumpled like piles of
giant cushions stuffed and
plumped to a deceptive softness -
covered by maple, hickory,
pine, beech and gum
glowing too green through air slightly
hazed and lit by an April sun.

The fertile smell of that maddening view
comes with spring in this place. And
the sounds of buzzing, chirping, trill and
caw, provide the music for a semi-tragic
opera which plays I think
just for me on this mammoth stage
once a year about this time.

Where I lie on the hill, the wind, that invisible seductress
with the sensual caress and monumental indifference,
joins the party to make worse the pain of a profound separation.

What is this anguish?
Why is the longing so visceral?
Must I burrow in the grass like a giant
vole pulling sod, soil and humus with pale root

tendrils and scurrying insects over my
head and rub them against
my face and body and smell the
mildewy aroma wafting up
from a soil busy resurrecting life
from the pieces of dead things?

Must I lie naked in sun or rain -
falling to roll in lush green grass
        to still find only a delusive
union with this aloof beauty

        Climb a tree, scrape against
        bark, even chew bitter leaves or
        lie in a brook with startled fish
        to scrabble for a corporeal sharing.
Stride across these bulging hillocks
Existing only in my jealous mind
stalking on illusory Bunyan legs
and groping with Promethean arms
to shovel to my brain
what my senses fail to provide,
to grab up and clasp the elements of this
scene tightly to see and smell
        and join it. Become it. Absorb it
into my being through the pores of my skin!
(Yes, imagine, imagine, imagine!
Another sense is needed!
Normal is not enough.
We should see joy and hear colors.
We should taste beauty and feel odors
and smell music.
We have not been given enough!)
Stop! I tell myself.

You will close those
giant arms on emptiness
and know again you have tried in vain.
Again too early for the union
and now, as ever,
gazing with hunger,
isolated, turned back to waiting,
understanding,
you truly join in this drama,
are a partner in this romance,
dance this dance, just once.
It will let you watch but
it will take you in
in only one way . . .
only when it is complete.

DREAMWORLD BUFFET

And then dream of
power over all you see
and meadow walks to violins.
Maybe the secret sweetness of perfect
revenge, or peace in the
world by wishing it so.
Oh, how you will impress your friends!
Or be a hero and save the threatened beauty
who falls into your arms.

Reshape lives like puzzle pieces
to make them fit
where you want them in
a world that you have designed.

Glory, beauty, wealth and fame
are laid out for the taking
at the Dreamworld buffet.

     Eat hearty, me lad,
for nothing remains at morning.
The trophy fish, medals and badges,
castles and joy, money and women
played with like toys in the darkness
disintegrate to bits of color,
a hopeless puzzle, fading fast
in the light of day;
like thrown confetti
to never, ever, go back

together again
but gathered like dust
and taken to the bin
or scattered on the ground,
blown away by the wind.

THE APPRENTICE BEGGER

The cold young boy roughly
asked for the coin, a bill,
anything, on the dirty

street embarrassed
that the need for the
money towered over the shame of this plea.

The thing he'd learned was to not
see the face and
the horror of his failure shining out of pitying eyes.

Got something,? he asked, hand out,
standing poised on one leg
looking down with the toes of the other

foot tapping just touching the
street as if testing a starting
block trembling and ready to

begin the run
away from the hated
hand to spend for a chemical

thing now so dear the
cost is measured in units of
pride lost in this place which

has only hard walls with emptiness
between. To run faster and faster,
panting and cursing

only to bounce from wall to wall to wall
inside this suffocating brick
box into which he was born
and fall and fall and fall,
beaten again

like a moth to a window sill
with battered, twitching wings
after fighting the window in the night
for the promise of the light.

BLUE COLLAR SORROW

Slapped, he was, on his dusty back;
his young and dirty shoulder
     in rough sympathy
     from oil-stained hands
     clumsy with anything but metal.
He'd had his day for her death
     but was now returned,
     on the job, faithful.
Money came first;
        pay the bills.

We'll drink a few beers, pal, they said.
     you'll soon get over it.
You got no choice,
     don' cha know.
Yet, he couldn't quite grasp
     the size of it . . .
     this first look at dying - the
completeness of it.

He didn't know how to tell them,
     that he felt too much,
     he could not
     make his words into their words.
     Didn't know what his face
     was supposed to do.
Didn't know how to play this part,
     ignore this much pain.

Among these pals,
      men of strength,
      who expected tough acceptance
like them when they suffered,
tracks of tears,
      it was understood,
on these dirty cheeks
      are marks of surrender.

NATURAL CAUSES

The report said
found, out in the wood,
fallen on leaves
where he often had stood.
Laid where he fell,
earth under head,
the report said natural,
two days dead.

No mention there
of memories stored
of children held
and wife adored.
No more words
for a life thus cropped;
something unplugged,
all systems stopped.

No evidence stayed,
not a trace,
of the lifetime played
at a dazzling pace
to sweeten his trip
to oblivion.

RUSTED WORDS

Steel cable bound still,
chained, fettered, wrapped,
welded, bolted, and riveted
(An iron chrysalis; no molting allowed.)
by the place of my birth.
> The very air of this nativity
> smelt of steel and oil,
> sweat, tobacco, and beer
> and was fogged blue
> by the smoke of the factory
> melting and forging parts
> of important American things.

Noble and needed,
this blast of the furnace,
the turn of the lathe,
and the skill of the
hand at a tool cutting steel.

Yet, even with that air, that smell
long gone and far away
(a young man escapes.)
all my words are often,
strained, and mashed
through this thick sieve,
> this coarse filter made
from those distant iron elements,
from that world of my youth,
jammed down now by tonnage
of expectations grown leaden

and squeezed out at the bottom
clanking on a gray steel tray
as blue metal pellets
which all feel the same;
identical, hard and cold.

IRONIC AUTUMN

By death transformed
but not by sorrow -
  rather a simple lack of ambient warmth
  and a secret signal
  borne through eons saying
  time to die.
The order is given.
Sweet fluids must be taken back
from the leafy crown
and banked for winter
beneath the ground below
  in the mirror tree
  spread regally there too
  but deep in soil
anchoring arches above.

  Leaves now transformed
  in nature's unique irony:
once green beauty alive, yes -
but a beauty greater in death.

Their lifesblood cut,
nothing rising from the banks below,
the curtains go up
with great fanfare
to open the show on
this autumnal abandonment.

  Brightly painted now
in a hundred stunning shades of
red, sienna, purple, orange and yellow.
  Totally dead.
There's naught to do
but cling and shine,
shimmy and shiver,
in time with autumn breezes
in defiance of this many-hued,
  splendid expiration.
Put on the show,
  break loose and fall,
  awkward now,
overcrisp, and smelling dry.
  Fragile.
  And, once fallen long enough
comes the ultimate irony;
rot to the sum of all colors;
the finality of black.
  Wait.

CLOTHES, SAYS CLYDE

Yep, you still see the sorriest men
there at the end.
      Same place for all, son,
      same place for all.
The biggest crook
and them who done
most terrible things
gonna float at peace
at the same place
'long side saints and angels
and you'll love 'em all.
      Cause
            life
is the treasure that
      goes to that final place.
Sins is jes' clothes.

FLOWER

Call down Chorydalis
Arraign the Orchidaceae
Indict the Indigo
And nab the Begonia
But the point of union
Of the blue and the deep, deep violet
Was the culprit in the latest abduction
All know that simple cells generate such perfection
But to search with cold reason and not the heart
By burrowing with metal tools to ever tinier parts
To where even molecules quiver
Shows no more than can be seen with the eye unhelped
And explains not a whit why such beauty dashes out and
Flashes its saucy crinolines to signal the time is ripe
For the wind to treat its progeny to a ride
Then too soon retreats behind its own curtains
And dies contentedly
In the unsentimental confines of its own inflexible schedule.
Simpler needs define it
Yet much larger needs are soothed by
This simple glowing presence
Nobler and ever more sadly beautiful
By the intense glory and wonder of its genesis
The sweet enigma of its existence reveals us
Which will applaud the creation
Which will mourn the passing

DON'T TELL ME I'LL BE FINE

A pepper just warm to a
tongue experienced can burn
like fire on the innocent palate.

An odor from nature can be a balm
to the nose which knows its source -
but revolting to the unaware.

Sorrow claimed sweet by the poet
is not so sugary to the soul
awash in its pain.

JUST A VISITOR

She was just a girl but thirty-seven
who said she could fly right out of the front
of her head and go
anywhere she wished. She went away
whenever she wanted
and was very pleased with herself.

She landed here once and visited for a while and I
was very happy though she didn't stay
long at all with so many places still to go.

I wondered what it looked like where
she went but she said no one can describe
the sky. It was a grand thing, she said,
to be able to leave the earth, but she told me
        I mustn't dream of such a thing
        because a person like me would
        never ever have wings.

CRIMES OF THE PAST

He commissioned the artist to paint
his face but not paint it darkly.
      He wanted the portrait
      to say he was sorry.
He hoped the painter would find
some good in his eyes which might
shine more brightly than the shadows
of things he had done.

But the only way, the artist said
with his knowing eye,
was to paint the word on
little scraps of gray paper and
paste them over everything
especially the eyes
making sure that nothing showed from
underneath.

POLITICIAN

I have stood with the stupid
moored with the morons
ideated with the idiots
sipped with the insipid
sinned with the sick
denned with the dense
drove with the dopes
lived with the liars
cried with the criers
gone with the goons
and laughed with the loons.

I have lain with the vain
vamped with the vapid
bragged with the boors
drooled with the fools
rutted with the rude
crowed with the crude
crawled with the crass
grubbed with the gross
veered with the vile
and made myself all the while

. . . smile.

APOLOGY

Blue eyes, good eyes, when I was small.
Now I say they seen it all.
Now folks lookin' at 'em seem aware
somethings wrong with the way I stare.
I can have my drink and swagger with a grin
yet none can see the shape I'm in.
Mostly I'm afraid how it's gonna come down.
I don't expect much, just to hang around.
But, I got what I wanted by doing the least.
It just don't count that I can't find peace
So I clown a bit when things don't seem right
and the jobs I do, I do out of sight
Who cares if I feel a little bad all the time.
Who cares if I don't have nothin' that's mine.
I can't cry and I wouldn't even if I could.
Can't laugh neither but if I could, I would.
Want to do something about my sore, aching gut.
Wine, whiskey and grease got it all tore up.
It don't bother me none to be so cold.
Won't hurt long cause I won't grow old.
Got no kin but my sis and my dad.
She's gone, ma's dead, and he's real bad.
I'm like him and he's like his son.
All we ever wanted was a drink and a gun.
It's only going to matter just a little while
that my eyes stay cold even when I smile.

THE TRICK

"Come here, come here, you must deny this!"
spake the wizened old man fiercely with words flashing
outward this time with the intensity of a laser beam.
"Come here, come here, you must hear me!
            I dare you to come here!"
    Thoughts blasted into space
by the fierceness, the enormity of the revelation,
this time struck the cloak of The Deus.

    Projecting his presence as
is his wont and special craft, once every few
centuries from where he reigns,
        from the blackness of space
        to the pretty blue ball
        to the whiteness of the clouds
        to the brown of a land form
        to the village of Ukgozrd near
        Mongolia to the stone and hide
        hut of Chatgaz Dzuunmond.

    Chatgaz sat next to the rough stone fireplace
        made with his own hands
and wove yarn, then blankets, from winter horse
hair and the fur of other creatures.
            He had much time to
think during the long, long winters
in the small stone hut he shared with his animals.
            And then he was not alone.
    "I am here," said The Deus, suddenly sitting

on Chatgaz' cot. Smiling.

     "You were laughing," said Chatgaz,
eyes widened in sudden awe
yet daring in his anger,

     "and it is not a good laugh.
Suddenly I saw you and I heard you laughing
and I am truly afraid that now I know why."

     "Why do I laugh?" asked The Deus,

     "You laugh because you tricked us," said Chatgaz.

     "And how did I trick you?" asked The Deus.

     "There is no hell," said Chatgaz. "There is no hell."
"Hell is your invention, not mine," said The Deus,
"I have no power to punish, only to bless.

     It makes me laugh that you find
     ever new ways to fear me
          when all I can do is love."
Chatgaz then laughed too, because, after all,

     The Deus was now laughing.
Chatgaz roared too at the import, the size, of this joke
though he knew what the world would be when

     this was understood.
And when he opened his eyes, he was alone again.
But there was a soft voice which remained, which said,
"You met me because you did not fear me.

     Listen to me:
I have no power to punish; only to bless.
Who would join me, would join me on that journey."

WRONG WIND

West wind howling
Bring me not those words which
Scream and cry before they die
Why dump this burden of sorrow
On my shoulders
When I am so ill equipped to
Bury them in this cold ground

You are cold blowing
This way – so cold
Blasting words like
Ice - cold and sharp
Able to pierce

Like ice they stab and hurt
Yet when gone, like ice
They leave no evidence
Of the crime   a puddle
Then soon no
Proof of guilt remains

These words and ice live
Together in that wind
Swooping in and out of open souls
Taking cold where
It should not go

A DAY BUILDING ROADS

Cloaked top to bottom in dirt and dust,
still cleaner than the shroud of cruelty
we also wore, we yipped in the
hot yellow air like hungry jackals smelling blood.

Tired grown men and a diesel-powered beast
pounded after a tiny mouse caught by bad fortune
and desperately bored laborers
on a flat open dirt table - acres across,
just stripped of all grass and shelter
and all things he called home.

We ran and stumbled in our big heavy boots
whooping and laughing
as we tried to stomp on this tiny creature
we were taught to abhor.

It ran and ran til we stood winded
and the mouse stood winded -
all stopped for a moment.
We might have been kind just then –
a moment of truce - but
the diesel beast roared
past me, wheels taller than my head.

I knew.
The mouse knew.
Done running, the mouse turned to face the beast
reared up on its hind legs, showed the claws
on his tiny paws
bared its teeth, and roared its anger
and fear, ready to fight a house-sized monster,
and died a bloody flattened hero.

I heard it, a scream at
all the world, ready to fight and die . . .
yet really just a squeak.

But I heard it and I remember it.
In all that noise I heard it.
And I heard the driver of the
beast roar with laughter.
He had won.   We had won.

With shame quickly brushed
from my shoulders by the happiness
and laughter of my brave fellow hunters,
I turned back to my shovel -
forever changed by a mouse,
a rodent,
because I could never,
ever forget such bravery.

MEMORIES OF SONS

Oh, you think I cringe like you
now you've grown
at the few mistakes you made
and wrong steps taken when you
were but babes.
But all you were was young.

Ah, the hollowness of your excuses
and the recount of your foibles is music
in my mind. They bring laughter,
not the anger you suspect.
For all you were was young.

And the clock which runs me and
will someday wind me down
finds such memories of your youth
and growth of wisdom
among the brightest lights in a mind
full of lights.
For once I too was young.

ANCESTRY

Which blood, I wonder, sears my veins?
And which blood cools their flow?
Which births a pulsing rage?
Which flows calm and slow?

A code infused through eons
Packed in brains and bones
Not learned - not planned
This wish for clubs and stones.

ABSTRACT STATUE

Lustrous marble
tucking hidden messages
in holes and curves
for puzzled viewers.

Good, It is saying;
You are here.
Welcome.
I am new to your eyes
with no parts on which to dwell -
no center, no beginning, no end.
I am easy to see
yet you must look hard to find me.
You must look with open eyes
and see all of me at once.

I am a new language:
You must listen with
new ears
and the words are words
you are speaking.
I am you or part of you
with different lines.

I have a way
        to tell you
how to believe, to think.
You can have the way
        and me.
        Touch me.
It is not true
that I am cold.

MELANCHOLY FARM

I step slowly though time and
ruin in a somehow majestic farmstead,
though now merely
brush-tangled wood and iron, and
kick aside dirt, rope and broken tools in a
lofty but half-roofed barn.
It seeps from metal, wood and stone . . .
this thickness of life once here sheltered.
        Cross a sunken back door
threshold into the paint peeled kitchen
and stumble over parts of chairs and
and creeping vines
        to open broken doors on cabinets,
shelves now home for mice
and a battered lunch box
which carried PBJ's for a schoolbound child.
Roy Rogers still smiles through the rust -
reins in hand ready to ride,
waiting for the young
hand grown old and gone.

DAVY GOT WINGS

Davy got wings and flew
the day he scored 54 points.
     His team won state.
     He flew and flew -
years and years above it all:
bad jobs, bad marriages, bad kids.
He still glided aloft . . .
even slept in the sky.

When things were bad,
wings getting weak,
an old classmate would say, "Man, I'll never
forget the night you scored 54 points.
You won state for us!" then buy another beer.
All would sigh at the glory of it,
and Davy would find new strength
and soar again, above it all.
Yeah, he would say, that was me, goddammit.
Yeah, I sure did it, didn't I.
     It was all he needed,
to stay aloft, be happy - still flying even if
nothing else was done with a sad life.
He had not touched the ground for years.
He had, after all, scored 54 points
and won state.

Then there was no one was left to
say the magic words.
The wings, lift gone,
        fluttered and folded
and Davy fell from the sky
        one night and landed
alone at the cheap plastic table
        in his little dirty kitchen
and found, back on the ground,
he could not walk again.

THE POLITICIANS

The driven man
With desperate eyes
Dances in the mine field
At the promise of power
In his wallet

The driven woman
With a cold cold smile
Dances with the devil
At the promise of power
In her pocketbook

A FINE CAR

I know there was a final check;
the last man with the clipboard
who said okay;
this car in which I am dying
could leave that plant
where robots had poked and jabbed its structure
making snapping, sparking welds
to make sure that it carried me safely -
that brought it all the way from there to here.
It is certainly not his fault
that this car is upside down,
wheels in the air, roof in the weeds.
It was just a moment of carelessness.

What a fine car!
Beautiful, with precise handling,
even a computer screen, you could touch
to make new commands
and brakes which would stop you on a dime.
We worked a long time to afford
a car like this.
Fine leather. Fine wood.

There was a moment, right at first,
of small regret at the blood
pooling on the beautiful headliner
beneath my head.

But my problems are much bigger than that.
I can not stop that bleeding
and I am getting very tired -
but strangely unconcerned.
I wish I could tell my family
that it was they who carried me.

A GOOD MAN

It's buried deep in the mind
of the god-fearing smiling
gentleman deacon elder
with easily proffered grip,
white smile, and warm hand.
          Off in that darkened corner
          hides a smelter - a
          cauldron always bubbling -
          melting bits and parts
          of life in this modern world -
          crafting new invisible alloys
          to stay current, to keep it
          hidden from the world,
hidden to all but like few -
these alloys unnamed: secret,
          but modern marvels;
shaped and molded to perfectly
create an open smiling facade
hiding the rage, hate and resentment
in a still cruel heart.

BILL AND THE BAR

There is no joy or songs being sung
in the dark of this beaten old bar
where watery rye and lifeless beer
are served in chipped fruit jars

Window grime and broken lights
shadow the slumping toper
marking his face like a mournful clown
and painting the walls dull ocher.

For many long years he sat alone
and swallowed anything brewed
with no thought at all for time gone by
and duty he drank to elude.

Deep anger once, and cruel things said,
were regrets long since ceased.
He once rode high but now rode low
and finally, with nothing, felt free.

BUMPKIN

Long ago I danced in a rustic old bar
with a sweet country girl.
I held her close to my chest
while I whispered
and she listened to me,
so smooth, so cool in black turtleneck,
way out in the hills
while the country men
stomped and glared at my certitude.

She trembled and sighed so pretty so fresh
and said she had never met anyone like me
but she was glad to have someone
       not like me.

I HOPE

I hope I know that death will come.
I hope I know when death will come.
I hope when death will soon be coming,
I hope I find that death's becoming.

BOY BORED

Bored to tears;
oatmeal with raisins
             again.
Bored with his mother's gentle pat
and kiss to the tousled hair
atop his morning head.
Bored again with the father's
reminder that he had to earn his tuition.
So mow the lawn today -
             or else.

Ran to sign up instead - excited about
the adventure. Then, in mere weeks,
looking at the place where his
leg had been;
light fading,
life fading.
All he wanted was
oatmeal with raisins.

GYPSY PROPHECY

You will not be the Ty
Cobb of awareness she told the actor,
laughing grimly at her poor humor,
peering into the glowing crystal orb
after a first look in a tent at the circus
wearing many scarves
and clinking silver bangles.

      Oh, yes, she said, now with a note of fear, I've found you.
      The light from others won't guide you.
      You will see only where your light shines.

Your flame will soon grow dim.
You'll have a long, long walk
alone in the dark, she said,
along the path you have chosen.

      Quickly she stood and held out her hand
      as if to touch him, calm him
      and he reached for it - now afraid.

That will be five dollars,
she said, quickly withdrawing her hand. Go now,
away from me. Do not ever return.
I do not touch such darkness.

THE SERVICE

Painfully pretty, pale silk floating down the stair,
      All white, like phosphorus, searing the air.

A perfect marriage, perfect daughter and groom,
      Flashback to hell in that deadly bloom.

White cake and laughter, champagne, singer,
      Tortured memory of a blown off finger.

Moved to a big house, the young man was loaded,
      He thought it was Powell, where the shell exploded.

The kids were so glad they had waited so long,
      Nothing else left, four guys just gone.

Both had careers, no kids in their plans,
      Blake thought it was Newsom, who had the black hands.

The whole world before them, to plan and begin,
      They argued in darkness whether it was burn or the skin

His daughter was happy, and his new son-in-law,
      They buried the finger, then cursed at it all.

They would have peace for all their lives,
      He can't find peace . . . no others survived.

BUY A SPOON

She painted cute faces
on cheap wooden spoons
in a booth at a fair
in Fort Wayne.

The faces all looked
like a child she had lost
but some, when she cried,
showed her pain.

FATHERS AND SONS

Their lives are marked on
the minds of sons - not
with pliant neb but
sharp chisel making
deep wrought signs so
clear never to disappear.
It's plain to see where
fathers marched
as giants, heralds, and heroes.

BATTLEFIELD

Fear was the air
Thick in panting lungs

Blood was the water
For the field's little flowers

Death was the gift
Opened in surprise

Flesh was the dirt
New food for worms

ANGER

Fields of flowers
      Flower fields,
How big a scythe
      Can a BIG man yield?

Cut he right
      Cut he left,
He still sees flowers
      At his death.

DARK AT THE MOUTH OF THE TUNNEL

Which way, then, now awakened to the need
to embark on this new journey I see before me:
the proper management of aging.

Right foot first, or left foot?
Remember the military sixty years ago.
      Basic training.
The drill sergeant's name was Prince.
(You thought I would forget.)

Will I have to walk all the way?
Can I ride some?
Will there be rocks along the path?
Suppose I stumble?
(You know these old ankles get weakish.)
But, first, stick to my plan.

Start with building that barrier behind the eyes
to block the troublesome images flashing
in the darkness of a tired mind:
the tastes, colors, sounds, smells,
of a robust younger life and strength, loves,
and, oh god, passion.

You can't see the darker road ahead
with eyes looking back at that sunny past.
      (That's not really helping.
      Turn your damned head around.)

Yes, dammit, I can do this myself.
I merely want someone to tell me
about the courage it takes, where it's found,

to grow old smiling, in peace,
to find a way to look without sorrow at
memories of the wild heart and bold voyages
of the younger man and shed all that fire
and accept the bland stillness of
a hobbled today.

I want someone who knows what to
do with things like this damned anger.
Where do I put it?
       Okay, I know.
            Behind me.
Just tell me where I am going.
Tell me how to do this.
Tell me the truth.

Start with the left foot.
Right?

RIDE TO CATATONIA

She went
      downhill, fast;
fast as if riding
on rails smooth as glass -
like floating backward, falling
yet not falling.
      No baggage on this trip.
Eyes wide, accepting just light,
      now on new terms.
Not allowing outside images in,
yet seeing only good images inside
in a mind just closed forever
to a world gone mad.
She once had a life so normal – good times.
A mother reading nursery rhymes.
Then came the knives and the murderous crimes.

This one will accept the fear, mud,
      carnage and blood
never, never more.
Only the touch of the wind,
the smell of her children's hair
      and flowers.
Only the sound of her children
laughing, and the taste of
honey and their skin are memories still alive
somewhere in a damaged core
now shielded by the salvation of insanity
from the poisonous barbs of modern cruelty

grown so common
they shot one day past her locks
into the heart of her home.

This mind does not compute wound and
gore.
It can no more hear the screams of pain
from a family slain.
No more.

LET'S GET REAL

You think I don't know
that what I'll do next
will always be done
in my own little context?

It's normal to see
that life's about me.
That what I will do
will follow that rule.

But, you think I will change
because I take the blame
for good things not done
and battles not won?

OLD MATH

I stand as one
Yet remain the sum
Of all I've seen
And all I've been

Good and bad
Joyous and sad
The total of fears
Then time, plus tears

TWIT WORD SELFIE

Usually I
think I
am right when I
see Me where I
put Myself and I
feel that I
should have what I
think is Mine even if I
know that maybe I
don't deserve it. I
don't think I
talk too much about Me. Do I?

HEARING AN FM APOLOGY TO JIM THORPE

Don't speak for me, you pup
In begging public recompense for slighted heroes of the past

The righteous bawling of sanctimonious
Self-appointed apologists misusing their media time

Who take it upon themselves
To say "I'm sorry" for me and generations

Of people who earned their tickets to life long ago
Tossing frothy "We were wrong's" into the air on FM or AM

To the long ago famed departed
Of course using first names as if somehow

The drift of these luminaries through eternity
Could be interrupted just long enough to get in

Just this one so unique message past the gates of wherever
The real shame is not in the wrong

Done to the few famous dead
The shame is in the failure to see the wrong in its place

After it fell onto the mountainous pile of misery
Just outside the door

Where the shreds from human
Cruelties are stacked and its ordinariness is so acceptable

The shame is in this juvenile blindness to
This towering heap of plain, boring, everyday anguish

Where the wrong done to heroes
Is lost on these bloody damned slopes of five and dime suffering

SEARCHING SOMEWHERE
FOR THE LONG GONE

God how afraid I am
to walk this quaking ground,
stalking an elusive wraith
through the endless maze in
my head while wary of pits and traps
which belong in another story yet
open so suddenly that
I jump as jagged memories pop
from old wounds along the edges
and stumble as wounded faces and
dead eyes are thrown under my feet
along this forced march it seems
                    I must take.
Yet stupidly I go on, one
foot after another,
                afraid to step,
        afraid to stop.
I know there's a door
but I don't know who closed it.
It wasn't me, I think.
        No, it was me.
Behind this door is a room
filled with childhood pain
locked in decades ago. Pain too
deep, too profound to
feel and survive back then.

You are there.
    I lost you when a child.
             I wasn't there.
You went under and, damn,
damn, damn, damn, damn
godammit.
I wasn't there.
I think I could have saved you.
      I.
      Wasn't.
      There.
Now I stand here older and wiser
      but still afraid to look.
Instead, I imagine your face
      in sunshine on the other side.
I still cannot feel goodbye.
How much of me does this explain?

MIRACLE CLOTH

Covered in blood, hung from poles
burned to ashes, shot full of holes

Casts a shadow under which men die
waved in joy, makes grown men cry.

Stuck in soil on some vague line
telling the world this side is mine.

A piece of cloth, a few colored bars,
a dark blue corner and a bunch of stars.

TWO CHOICES

I knew a man whose life was enclosed
  in a circle too small for his art.

I knew a woman whose heart was put in a box
  and hid away until she was too old to open it.

I knew a girl who gave herself too soon and too often
  and found she could not get herself back.

I knew a boy whose hopes were scattered from the start
  and never found a way to put them back together.

Each found a way to float
  on those tides which would consume them.

AUTUMN LEAVES

We are small but many.
We are so many that
the impact of our
gathered beauty
strikes the eye again
in surprise like a new thing
year after year.
We are seen best from afar
with each tree and bush
like a separate brilliant leaf
on a mountain-sized spray
in beautiful array.

But, look, it's time again.
         We are gone
and you must wait now
'til another season pushes
sprouts from stalk and limb.
The time of our leaving,
cannot be changed
by the wish that we
remain on stage
         and always so pretty.

KNIVES, MATCHES AND MEDICINE

A child should be taught
at an early age that words are like
      knives with sharp
      edges that slice
if pulled from the
scabbard and carelessly thrown
leaving cuts that never heal.

A child should learn from an early age
that words are like
matches when struck
      making fire
 which cannot be quenched
      burning those too close
leaving scars which last a lifetime.

A child should be taught from an early
age that words are like medicine,
like the rarest cures able
to quickly heal lacerations
salve and cool the burns
and wipe away scars.

LOST

The person born with
a broken compass
flops like a fish
abandoned on a muddy flat
by the ebb and flow of life
wondering how
others so easily remained
in the stream and found the
oxygen needed to survive.

The person born with
a broken compass
searches over and over on
shelf after shelf for that book
with all the definitions and
directions on things one must do
to be complete and wonders
how others so easily found it.

NOT MY FAULT

I fooled everyone who
thought it was me who said
the things in my mind.

None could tell that it was the image
of me wandering around in my clothes
in my shoes in my house just nattering.

I meant to tell the truth
all along but he wasn't here
at the right time to spit it out.

But anyway the truth is mere humor,
another story told from the fingers
of this me shape

and too boring to make me take the blame
and neither of us could tell which is worse,
failure in prose or failure in verse.

FAILED POET

Some words got loose
which were not obtuse
but instead, I fear,
were perfectly clear

FRIDAY

In luck I sit at lunch with men,
all of whom I admire.
Gathered at this table round
are wisdom, truth, and fire.

PUNCTU

vowels consonants
syllables words paragraphs
stuck together with pitiful glue
tumble off the edge
of this mental precipice
land on paper
stop
words crawl across the page
pause
words crawl across the page
longer pause
words crawl across the page
change
words crawl across the page
stop
damn
tumble away
-ATION

CONREMODEMPROCRAT

Search right and left
along this bent line -
find no pol correct
even half the time

All's left is independent
and stick with this view:
trust in the old
and pray for the new.

GNU LAWS

If gnus are outlawed
Only outlaws will own gnus!

AFTERWORD

The process of writing is somehow compelling, and the need to do it will not go away. Hence this collection of thoughts and images, using words which sometimes rhyme, to express dismay, anger, humor, and parts of a personal philosophy. I am not a poet. I have too much respect for the art and discipline of poetry to claim that I am. I love words and I love to use words and it would be nice if someone else enjoyed reading what I wrote. That would be enough. In fact, Samuel Johnson says I am a blockhead. He said that "No man but a blockhead ever wrote except for money."

Though it may be difficult to discern at times, this is all about life. I am fascinated by the world around me, both human and natural. I see tragedy and there is always a story. I see beauty and literally ache at the sight of it. I view these things in a peculiar way and try to describe what I see; sometimes poorly, I know. While I believe in the goodness of most people, I want to include the bad along with the good. Bad happens to people. People do bad things. Certainly this is no revelation. Yet offering a different way to look at it might be a worthwhile contribution.

While working my way through college, I was a waiter in a restaurant where a Viet Nam veteran bartended. I was also a veteran. As veterans, we got along well and related our different experiences. He told of the times as a medic on a helicopter where it would happen too often that, after they brought aboard wounded soldiers during the heat of battle, bullets would come up through the bottom of the chopper and further wound or kill the men as he was frantically working to save them. Now he was just another student working his way through college. He never talked about his own heroism. But, in that Ohio restaurant, he just shook his head and laughed at this experience in war and served another drink.

That laugh has stayed with me many decades later. It certainly wasn't humor. How can you laugh at such tragic, stupidly ironic death which occurs in a violent way in the midst of incredibly heroic actions? The answer, of course, is that you have to. He had to. He had to because of the insanity of it all; to keep from being overcome by anguish and bitter frustration. However, I don't think there are enough words in any language to ever be able to adequately describe this response to cruel death in the midst of unbelievable gallantry. There are so many levels of humanity and life embodied in that extraordinary expression that words will never be able to convey it by themselves alone. So, words cannot truly re-create the reality of even one simple little chuckle. What I love about reading and writing is the ongoing attempt to try it anyway. We want to see what we can do with words. We want to see what words will do.

Years ago, I read about persons who had supposedly died for a brief period and came back from wherever they had briefly gone with a simple lesson for living. Many concluded from this extraordinary experience that there is a most profound and simple philosophy for living: that the best things we could do with our lives are to keep learning and do good things. That seems so simple, yet so fundamental. I try to do both. I have learned a lot. I wrote this little book about some of it. I hope that is a good thing.

CPSIA information can be obtained at www.ICGtesting.com
Printed in the USA
BVOW02*0517170216

437020BV00002B/40/P

9 781478 759386